Street by Stre

C000177610

READING

HENLEY-ON-THAMES, WOKINGHAM

Burghfield, Caversham, Goring, Mortimer, Pangbourne, Sonning Common, Spencers Wood, Theale, Tilehurst, Twyford, Wargrave, Winnersh, Woodley

3rd edition September 2007
© Automobile Association Developments Limited 2007

Original edition printed May 2001

 This product includes map data licensed from Ordnance Survey® with the permission of the Controller of Her Majesty's Stationery Office. © Crown copyright 2007. All rights reserved. Licence number 100021153.

Published by AA Publishing (a trading name of Automobile Association Developments Limited, whose registered office is Fanum House, Basing View, Basingstoke, Hampshire RG21 4EA. Registered number 1878835).

Produced by the Mapping Services Department of The Automobile Association. (A03387)

A CIP Catalogue record for this book is available from the British Library.

Printed by Oriental Press in Dubai

The contents of this atlas are believed to be correct at the time of the latest revision. However, the publishers cannot be held responsible or liable for any loss or damage occasioned to any person acting or refraining from action as a result of any use or reliance on any material in this atlas, nor for any errors, omissions or changes in such material. This does not affect your statutory rights. The publishers would welcome information to correct any errors or omissions and to keep this atlas up to date. Please write to Publishing, The Automobile Association, Fanum House (FH12), Basing View, Basingstoke, Hampshire, RG21 4EA. E-mail: *streetbystreet@theaa.com*

Ref: ML055y

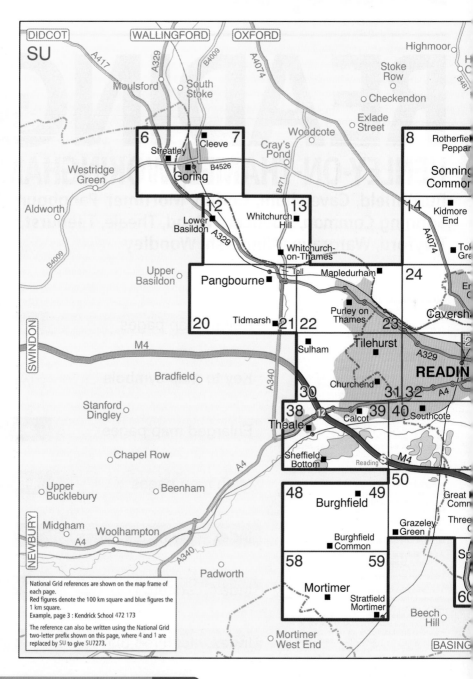

DIDCOT WALLINGFORD OXFORD

SU

A417 A329 B4009 A4074

Highmoor

Stoke Row

Moulsford South Stoke Checkendon

Exlade Street

Westridge Green

Woodcote

6 Cleeve **7** Cray's Pond

Streatley

Goring B4526

Aldworth

B4009

8 Rotherfie Peppar

Sonning Common

14 Kidmore End

A4074

Tol Gre

12 Whitchurch Hill **13**

Lower Basildon A329

Whitchurch-on-Thames

Upper Basildon

Toll

Pangbourne Mapledurham

24 En C

20 Tidmarsh **21** **22** Purley on Thames **23** Caversh

Sulham Tilehurst

A329

Bradfield

M4

A340

Churchend

READIN

30 **31** **32** A4

Stanford Dingley

Chapel Row

A4

38 **39** **40**

Theale 12 Calcot Southcote

Sheffield Bottom Reading

M4

Upper Bucklebury

Beenham

50 Great Comm

Midgham Woolhampton

A4 A340

48 **49** Burghfield

Grazeley Green Three C

Burghfield Common

Padworth

58 **59** Sp

Mortimer Stratfield Mortimer

Beech Hill

SWINDON NEWBURY

60

Mortimer West End BASING

National Grid references are shown on the map frame of each page.
Red figures denote the 100 km square and blue figures the 1 km square.
Example, page 3 : Kendrick School 472 173

The reference can also be written using the National Grid two-letter prefix shown on this page, where 4 and 1 are replaced by SU to give SU7273.

Enlarged scale pages 1:10,000 6.3 inches to 1 mile

0 1/4 miles 1/2

0 1/4 1/2 kilometres 3/4 1

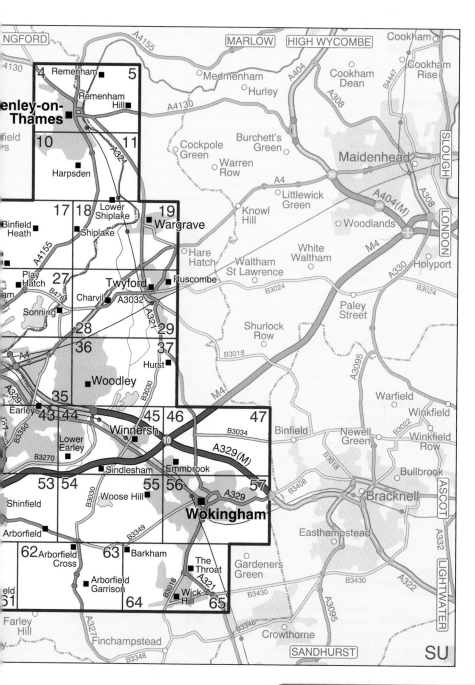

NGFORD

A4155

MARLOW   HIGH WYCOMBE   Cookham

A4130

4 Remenham   5

Medmenham
Hurley

Cookham
Dean

Cookham
Rise

A404

enley-on-
Thames

Remenham
Hill

A4130

B4447

SLOUGH

field
s

10   11

Harpsden

A321

Cockpole
Green

Burchett's
Green

Warren
Row

A308

Maidenhead

A4

Littlewick
Green

A4130

9B

A404(M)

A308

LONDON

17 18 Lower
Shiplake

19

Wargrave

Binfield
Heath

Shiplake

Knowl
Hill

Woodlands

M4

White
Waltham

5A

A4155

A321

Hare
Hatch

Waltham
St Lawrence

A330

Holyport

Play
Hatch

27

Twyford

Ruscombe

B3024

B3024

am

B478

Charvil

A3032

Sonning

28   29

36   37

Hurst

A321

Shurlock
Row

Paley
Street

B3018

A3095

Woodley

B3030

M4

35

Earley

A329

43 44 45 46   47

Winnersh

10

A329(M)

Warfield

Winkfield

Binfield

Newell
Green

Winkfield
Row

B3022

B3350

B3270

Lower
Earley

Sindlesham

Emmbrook

B3018

Bullbrook

ASCOT

53 54 55 56 57

Woose Hill

A329

Bracknell

Shinfield

B3030

Wokingham

B3349

Arborfield

Easthampstead

B3408

A332

62 Arborfield
Cross

63 Barkham

The
Throat

Gardeners
Green

A321

B3430

A322

LIGHTWATER

A327

Arborfield
Garrison

B3016

64 65

A321

Wick
Hill

B3430

A3095

eld
61

Farley
Hill

A327

Finchampstead

B3348

Crowthorne

SANDHURST

SU

B3348

4.2 inches to 1 mile   **Scale of main map pages 1:15,000**

0   1/4   miles   1/2   3/4   1

0   1/4   1/2   kilometres 3/4   1   1 1/4   1 1/2

Symbol	Description	Symbol	Description
Junction 9	Motorway & junction	LC	Level crossing
Services	Motorway service area		Tramway
	Primary road single/dual carriageway		Ferry route
Services	Primary road service area		Airport runway
	A road single/dual carriageway		County, administrative boundary
	B road single/dual carriageway		Mounds
	Other road single/dual carriageway	17	Page continuation 1:15,000
	Minor/private road, access may be restricted	3	Page continuation to enlarged scale 1:10,000
←	One-way street		River/canal, lake, pier
	Pedestrian area		Aqueduct, lock, weir
	Track or footpath	465 Winter Hill	Peak (with height in metres)
	Road under construction		Beach
	Road tunnel		Woodland
P	Parking		Park
P+	Park & Ride		Cemetery
	Bus/coach station		Built-up area
	Railway & main railway station		Industrial/business building
	Railway & minor railway station		Leisure building
⊖	Underground station		Retail building
⊖	Light railway & station		Other building
+++++++++	Preserved private railway		

⊓⊔⊓⊔⊓⊔⊓	City wall		♜	Castle
A&E	Hospital with 24-hour A&E department		🏛	Historic house or building
PO	Post Office		Wakehurst Place NT	National Trust property
📖	Public library		M	Museum or art gallery
i	Tourist Information Centre		♞	Roman antiquity
i	Seasonal Tourist Information Centre		⊥	Ancient site, battlefield or monument
▮ ▮	Petrol station, 24 hour Major suppliers only		🏭	Industrial interest
†	Church/chapel		✳	Garden
👫	Public toilets		◉	Garden Centre Garden Centre Association Member
♿	Toilet with disabled facilities		🌹	Garden Centre Wyevale Garden Centre
PH	Public house AA recommended		🌳	Arboretum
🍴	Restaurant AA inspected		🛒	Farm or animal centre
Madeira Hotel	Hotel AA inspected		🦌	Zoological or wildlife collection
🎭	Theatre or performing arts centre		🦅	Bird collection
🎥	Cinema		🦆	Nature reserve
⚑	Golf course		🐟	Aquarium
▲	Camping AA inspected		V	Visitor or heritage centre
🚐	Caravan site AA inspected		Ψ	Country park
▲🚐	Camping & caravan site AA inspected		⌒	Cave
🎡	Theme park		✖	Windmill
🏛	Abbey, cathedral or priory		🛢	Distillery, brewery or vineyard

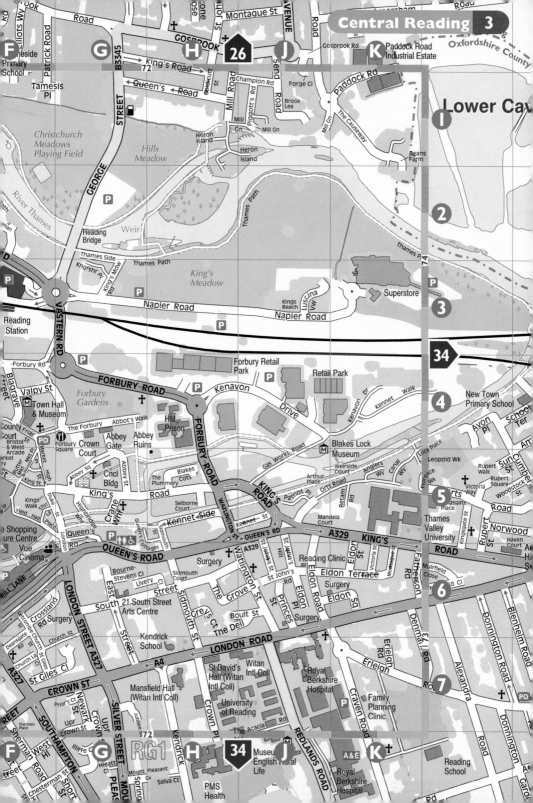

E   F   G   H

77   78

Temple Island

Remenham Lane

Remenham

✝

1
Aston

Aston Ferry Lane

84

Thame

Culham

2

Remenham
Church

Remenham
Court

Lane

3

Common
Barn

Aston Lane

Remenham
Place

**Remenham
Hill**

83

4

HILL

dlands

Matson Drive   WHITE

A4130

Park
Place

Aspect Park
Golf Centre

Golf Course

5

82

A321

es Stn

ames Path

M River & Rowing
Museum at Henley
& Wind in the Willows

77   78

ow E   F   GRAVE II   G   H

Fairview
Trading
Estate

Henley Town
FC

Lane

6

A B C D

458 59

82

1

Thurle
Grange

WANTAGE

ROAD

WALLINGFORD

Streatley
Farm

ROAD

Rectory   Road

Goring &
Streatley
Golf Club

Townsend Road

Lane

Three Gables

Lough
Down

A417

2

81

Golf Course

Streatley

The
Swan
Hotel

Surgery

3

STREATLEY HILL   B4009

The Bull
Mdw

Hill Gdns

HIGH   STREET

Streatley
CE Primary
School

The Coombe

READING

Thames Rd

Ferry Lane

Grange Close

The
Beeches

4

80

A329

5

Thames

458 59

A B C D

Wood Farm

Stichens
Green

A329

1 grid square represents 500 metres

Spring Farm

Beech Lane

County

E **F** **G** **H**

61 62

82

Icknield Road

Wroxhills Wood **I**

West Way

Springhill Road

Middle Springs

Cleeve

Elvendon

Road

Icknield Pl

Cleeve Down

Summerfield Rise

Battle Road

Road

CIV Dwn

Goring CE Primary School

Cleeve Down

Milldown Road

2

81

Heron Shaw

Lycroft Cl

Fairfield Road

Milldown Av

Ferne Cl

Lockstile Md

Lockstile Way

Meadow Cl

READING ROAD B4526

3

Valley Cl

Farm Rd

Upr Red Cross Rd

Whitehills Gn

Burntwood

GORING

Goring & Streatley Station

Great Chalk Wood

4

Holmlea Road

Elmcroft

Gatehampton Road

Upper Gatehampton Farm

80

5

Gatehampton Manor

Gatehampton Road

Thames Path

E **F** **12** **G** **H**

61 62

River Thames

Church Farm

Thames Path

8

A B C D

Lime Avenue

Stoke Row Road

Stevens La

Stevens Lane

Dove La

1

82

468

69

merhedge Wood

Wyfold Grange

2

Wyfold Lane

Nippers Grove

81

3

Reades Lane

New Copse

Horsepond Road

4

Withy Copse

Gallowstree Common

Woodside La

Hearns La

Bishopsw

The Hamlet

Horsepond Road

Reade's Lane

180

5

Hazelmoor Lane

READING ROAD

Wood Lane

468

A

B

▼**14**

C

D

Cane End Farm

Wood Lane

aysleaze

Cane End

Kidmore End

Kidmore End CE Primary School

1 grid square represents 500 metres

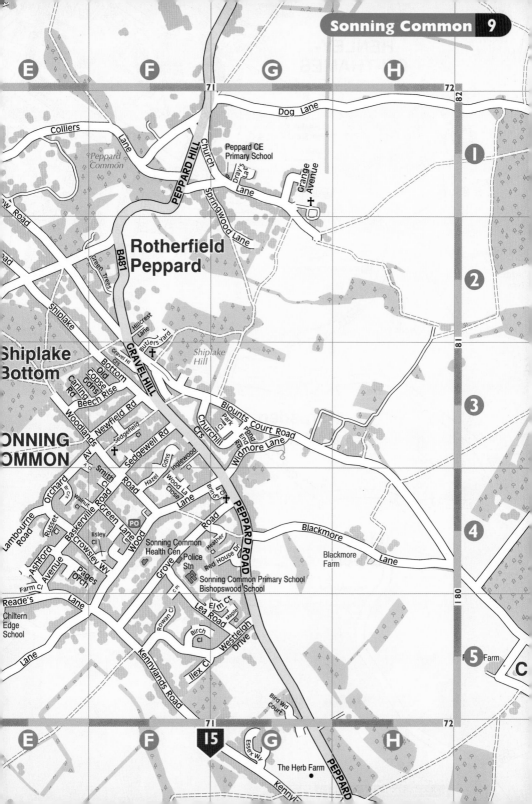

E F G H

1
2
3
4
5

72
82
81
80

Dog Lane

Colliers Lane

Peppard Common

PEPPARD HILL

Church Hill

Peppard CE Primary School

Draytes Lane

Springwood Lane

Grange Avenue

Rotherfield Peppard

B481

Green Trees

Shiplake

Hillcrest Lane

Butlers Yard

GRAVEL HILL

Gravel Hill

Shiplake Hill

Blounts Court Road

Shiplake Bottom

Bottom

Old Copse Gdns

Carling Rd

Beech Rise

Woodlands

Newfield Rd

Sedgefield Ct

Park End

Pond End

Widmore Lane

Churchill Cres

SONNING COMMON

AV

smith Ct

Sedgewell Rd

Hazel Gdns

Inglewood Cl

Wood La

Brays Cl

Orchard

Russet Cl

Baskerville Rd

Walnut Ct

Green Lane Wood

Ilsley Cl

Crowsley Wy

Sonning Common Health Cen

PO

PEPPARD ROAD

Blackmore Lane

Blackmore Farm

Lambourne Road

Ashford Avenue

Pages Orch

Farm Cl

Reade's Lane

Chiltern Edge School

Grove Road

Police Stn

Heather Cl

Red House Dr

Sonning Common Primary School
Bishopswood School

Elm Ct

Maple Cl

Lea Road

Rowan Cl

Birch Cl

Westleigh Drive

Kennylands Road

Ilex Cl

5 Farm

C

15

Essex Wy

The Herb Farm

Kennyl

PEPPARD ROAD

Bird Wd Court

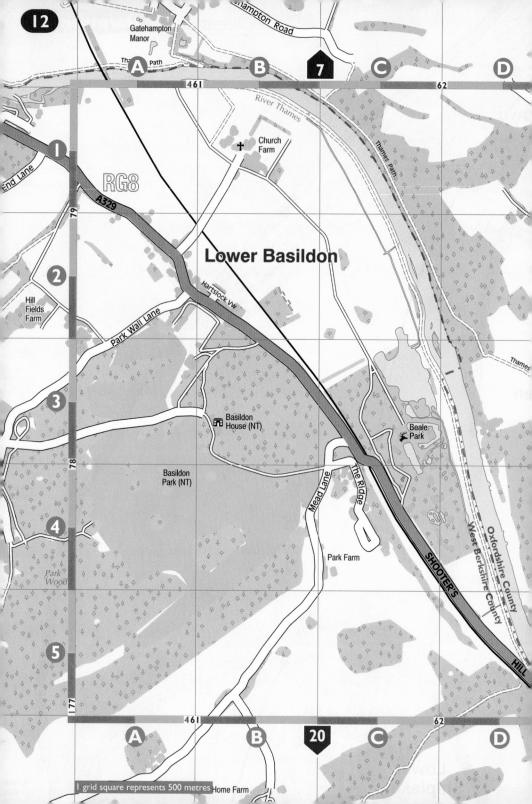

Lower Basildon

12

7

20

A B C D

461 62

RG8

End Lane

A329

79

Thames Path

Gatehampton Manor

hampton Road

River Thames

Church Farm

Thames Path

Hartslock vw

Park Wall Lane

Hill Fields Farm

78

Basildon House (NT)

Basildon Park (NT)

Park Wood

77

Mead Lane

The Ridge

Park Farm

Beale Park

SHOOTER'S

HILL

Oxfordshire County

West Berkshire County

Thames

461 62

A B C D

1 grid square represents 500 metres

Home Farm

1

2

3

4

5

E   F   G   H

63   64

Hill Bottom

Gashes La

Hocketts Cl

Hill Bottom Cl

Rivacres

B471

Oakdown Cl

Coombe End Farm

Orchard Coombe

Bridle Road

Beg Tithe

79

Whitchurch Hill

1

Butlers Pond

2

Beech Farm

Bozedown House

3

78

Hartslock

4   Hardwick

Bridleway

Bozedown Farm

Hillside

Hardwick   Road

B471

Swanston Field

Whitchurch Primary School

Eastfield Lane

Manor   Road

177

Whitchurch-on-Thames

5

Eastfield   Lane

HIGH STREET

E   F   G   H

63   64

A329

21

Toll

Hartslock Court

Pangbourne Medical Centre

CHURCH RD

Thames Path

Thames

School
Lane
Ilex Cl
Westley Drive
Bir Cl
Kennylands Road

E **F** **9** **G** **H** C

71 72

Essex Wy
Wd Court

The Herb Farm

Kennylands Road

PEPPARD

I

79

ROAD

2

Chalkhouse
Green Road

Vines Farm

Chalkhouse

Green

Road

Dysonswood Lane

Dyson's
Wood

Chalkhouse Green

Lane

B481

Bishop

3

16

78

**Chalkhouse
Green**

RG4

Dysonswood
La

Dysonswood Lane

Tanners Lane

Kidmore End Road

Chalkhouse
Go Lane
The
Ridings

Phil
Tower

4

Tanner's Farm

Tanners Lane

PEPPARD

Peppard Rd

Rose
Park

5

Crawshay Dr
Greenleas
Avenue
Olson Cl
Crawshay Dr

Jefferso
Cl

ROAD

Golf Course

Brooklyn
Dr

Courtenay
Dr

Burnham
Rise

Kidmore End Road

Twin
Oaks

Yarnton
Cl

Wetherby
Cl

E **F** **25** **G** **H**

71 72

down Avenue

Albany Gdns

Hig...

Grave/Hl
Old
Barn Cl

Eric Av

Reading
Golf Club

Chalgroves
Wy

St Benets

**Emmer
Green**

Gravel Hill
Wint...

Hafod
Aberan

Merthyr
Rd

venfeld Ct

Dunster

16

Frieze Farm

Crowsley

A
B
C
D

472
73

79

B481

1

2

3

15

78

Coppid Hall

Bishopsland Farm

Comp Farm

Gravel

Cork's Farm

Sandpit Lane

Chalkhouse on Lane

Phillimore Rd

Tower Cl

The Ridings

Russet Gdns

Marchwood Av

Autumn Cl

Cherry Cl

Bryant's Farm

Kiln Road

Row

Church Lane

Lane

Church Lane

Dunsden Green

Rosehill Park

PEPPARD

Peppard Rd

Venetia Close

Jefferson Cl

Kiln Road

Foxhill Lane

Crenshaw Dr

Greenacre Avenue

Greenleaf

Stimpson Cl

Brooklyn Dr

Courtenay Dr

ROAD

Farnton Cl

Burcot Ln

Twin Oaks

Chalgrove Wy

Kidmore End Rd

Wetherby Cl

Br Cl

Queensway

Pendennis

Caversham Park Road

Rowallan

Caversham Park Primary Sch

St Martins RC Prim Sch

472

73

26

A
B
C
D

Reading Golf Club

Canfield Ct

4

5

77

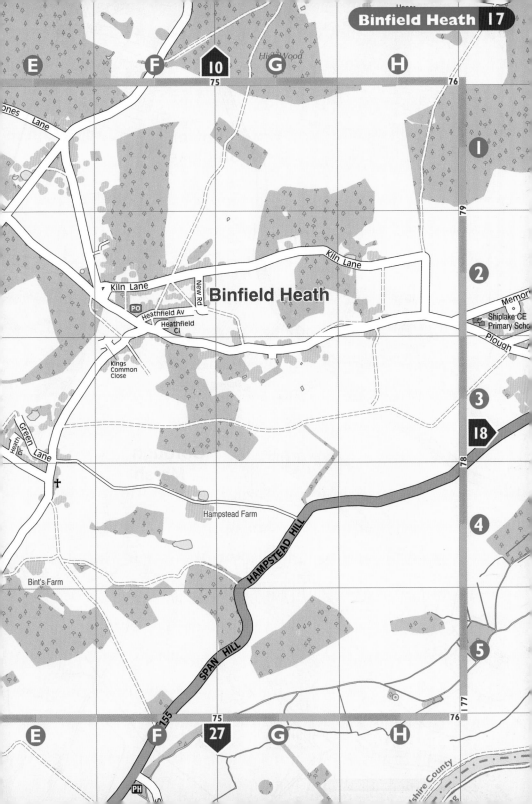

Upper

E   F   **10**   G   H

75   76

I

ones Lane

79

Kiln Lane

Kiln Lane

New Rd

Binfield Heath

2

Memor

Shiplake CE
Primary Scho

PO
Heathfield Av

Heathfield
Cl

Plough

Kings
Common
Close

3

18

Green Lane

Heath Dr

78

✝

Hampstead Farm

4

HAMPSTEAD HILL

Bint's Farm

5

SPAN HILL

177

155

75   76

E   F   **27**   G   H

PH

shire County

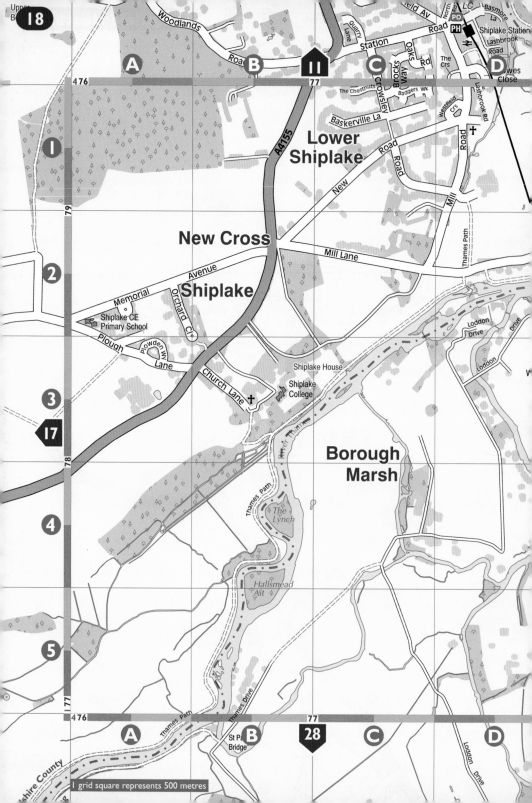

E   F   G   H

Willow Lane

WARGRAVE ROAD

79

80

I

79

Wargrave Manor

The Copse   Dunnock Way

Blakes   Road

Hanover Gdns

Highfield Park

Blakes Road

Highfield Park

Blakes Road

2

Ridge Way

The Bothy

A321

PH

Wargrave Hill

The Walled Gdn

Hill Lands

Ridge Wy

Lantana Wy

Dark Lane

Autumn Wk

Backsideans

PO

Ferry La

Church St

watermans Wy

Station Road

WARGRAVE

Braybrooke

Bayliss Rd

Braybrooke Gdns

Spring Walk

Wk

HIGH STREET

SCHOOL LANE

B477   SCHOOL HILL

Ricroft

Newalls Ri

Fidlers Walk

Purfield

Surgery

Victoria

Emma Rd

Hamilton Rd

Silverdale Rd

Beverley

Gdns

Clifton Rl

Road

East Vw

Rd

Recreation Rd

Newalls Ri

East VW

East VW

PO

Harvest Pl

The Robert Piggott CE Junior School

The Robert Piggott CE Infant School

Kingswood House

3

MUMBERY HILL

78

B477

A4 BA

Sheeplands Farm

4

BATH   ROAD

NEW   WAY

A4

A3032

The Piggott School

Wargrave Road

Malvern Way

Badger Dr

New

Road

Hilltop

Heron Dr

5

177

Castle

WARGRAVE

A321

Carlile Gdns

Chaseside Av

Kewhurst Cl

Salix Gdns

Llewellyn Pk

Longfield

E   F   **29**   G   H

Kimberley Av

Longfield Road

Troutbeck

Jarvis Cl

Willow

Heron Dr

Pennfields

Crest Cl

Middlefields

London Rd

Walnut Tree Close

Northbury Farm

New

End Rd

79

80

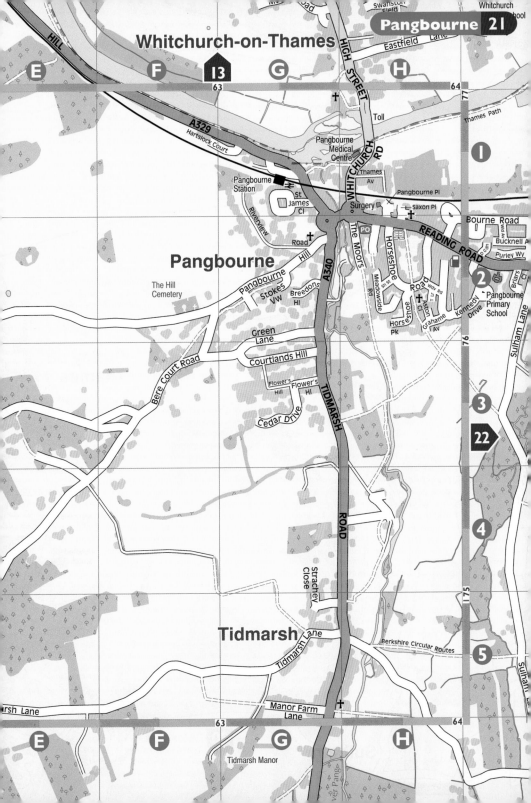

Whitchurch-on-Thames

E F 13 G H

63 64 77

A329

Hartslock Court

HILL

HIGH STREET

Swanston Field

Whitchurch

Eastfield Lane

Toll

Pangbourne Medical Centre

Thames Av

Thames Path

I

Pangbourne Station

St James Cl

Surgery

Pangbourne Pl

Saxon Pl

WHITCHURCH RD

READING ROAD

Bourne Road

Bucknell A

Purley Wy

Riverview Road

Pangbourne

Pangbourne Hill

Stokes Vw

Breedons Hl

The Moors

PO

Horseshoe Road

Meadowside

Horseshoe Pk

Aston

Grahame Av

Kennedy Drive

2

Pangbourne Primary School

Briars

The Hill Cemetery

A340

Green Lane

Courtlands Hill

Flower's Hill

Flower's Hl

Cedar Drive

76

Sulham Lane

3

22

Bere Court Road

TIDMARSH ROAD

4

Strachey Close

175

Tidmarsh

Tidmarsh Lane

Berkshire Circular Routes

5

Manor Farm Lane

Sulham

rsh Lane

63 64

E F G H

Tidmarsh Manor

River Pang

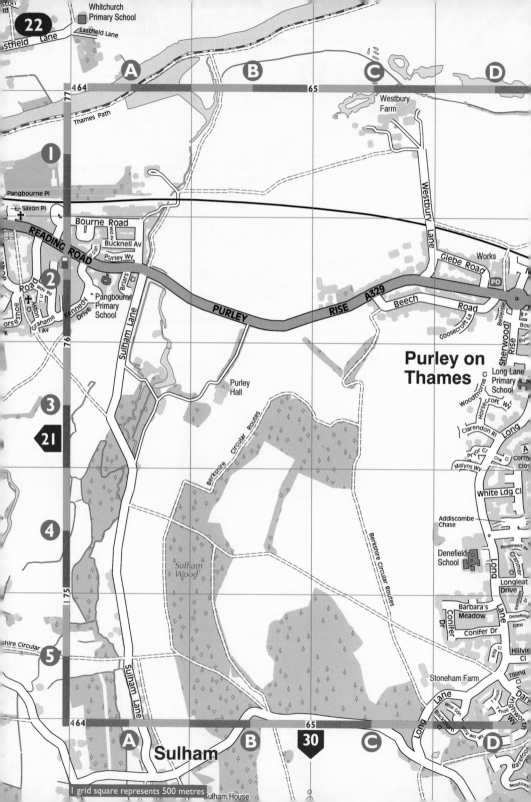

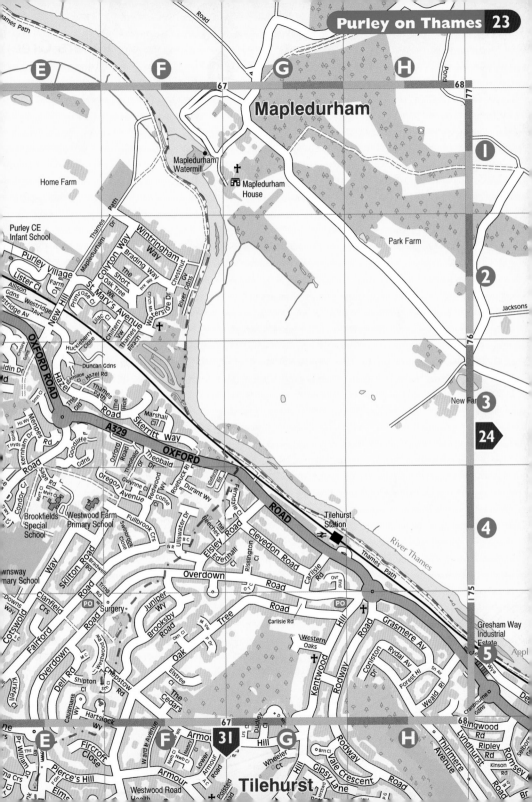

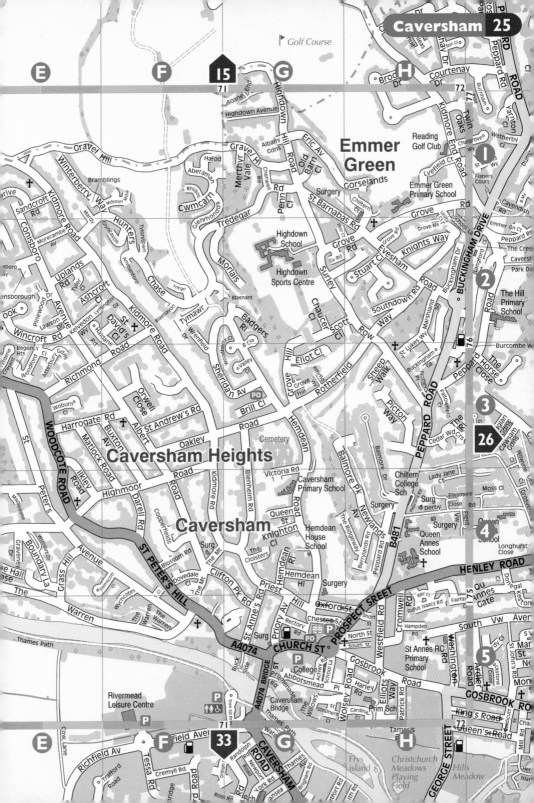

Golf Course

E F **15** G H

71 72

Emmer
Green

Reading
Golf Club

Emmer Green
Primary School

I

Highdown Avenue
Soane's End
Highdown
Hill Road
Albany
Gdns
Eric Av
Old
Barn
Cl

Broo Dr
Courtenay
Burnham
Yarnton
Cl
Peppard Rd
ROAD
Spn Cl
Twin
Oaks
Chalgrove
Wy
St
Wetherby
Cavendish
Dun
Fishers
Court

Gravel Hill
Winterberry Way
Bramblings
Hafod
Aberaman
Rhlos
Cwmcarn
Merthyr
Vale
Gravel Hi
Tredegar
Penn
Cl
Cherwell
Rd
Gdns
St Barnabas Rd
Surgery
Gorselands
Chiltern
Grove
Grove Rd
Grove Ms
Unity
Knights Way
Emmer Gn Ct
The Cres
Caversh
Park Dr
Kidmore End Rd
Langford

Buckingham Dr

BUCKINGHAM DRIVE
Langford
Rd
Emmer
Gn La
Peppard Rd
2

The Hill
Primary
School

Sandcroft
Rd
Consboro
Morcambe
Av
Hunters
Chase
Marcy
Armanford
Blaenavon
Dr
Tregyn
Tvorstrom
Glenrhondd
Blaenant
Highdown
School
Highdown
Sports Centre
Surley
Grove
Rd
Gv Rd
Stuart Cl
Chesham
Southdown Rd
Marshland
76
Peppard
Road
Burcombe W
The Horse Close
3

Regency
Hts
Woodford
Artfebury
Gdns
Uplands
Rd
Pinewood
Lawson
Dr
Avenue
Kelvedon
Wy
Lymington
ca
Haldane
St's
David's
Cl
Kidmore Road
Ashcroft
Richmond
Road
Tymawr
Wrenfield
Dr
Trfrgn
Badgers
Rl
B Clo
Valley
Grove Hill
Eliot Cl
Rotherfield
St Lukes Wy
Buckingham
Fallowfield
Sheep
Walk
Cedar Wd
Cl
Cavsm
Gdns
The
Cl
26
Islan
Cl

Wincroft Rd
ensborough
Kidmore
Road
Sheridan Av
Orwell
Close
St Andrew's Rd
Brill Cl
Hemdean
Grove
Hill
PO
Picton
Way
Balmore
Dr
4

WOODCOTE ROAD
Harrogate Rd
Matlock Road
Buxton
Av
Albert
Oakley
Road
Highmoor
Darell Rd
Kidmore Rd
Blenheim Rd
Cemetery
Victoria Rd
Caversham
Primary School
Balmore Pk
Chiltern
College
Sch
Lady Jane
Ct
Surg
Derby
Moss Cl
Ellesmere
Close
Surgery
Queen
Annes
School
Longhurst
Close

Caversham Heights

Ilkley
Road
Copperfields
Blossom Rd
Dovedale
Caversham
Queen
St
Knighton
Cl
The
Cloisters
Hemdean
House
School
The Ridgeway
Newlands
Surgery
B481
Queen
Annes
Gate

Peter's
Grassa
Hill
Avenue
Kelmscott
Wychcotes
The
Warren
The Warren
ST PETER'S HILL
Clifton
Pk
Rd
The Mt
Priest
Hill
Priory Av
Hemdean
Rl
Hemdean
Hl
Surgery
Oxford St
Berrylands Rd
Peppard Road
PROSPECT STREET
HENLEY ROAD
Rufus Isaacs Rd
Fairfax
Cromwell
Rd
Donegal
Keston
South Vw
Aver
Mar
St
Ne

Boundary La
Warren Dr
Graveney
Dr
The
Hall
se
The
Richmead
Leisure Centre
Thms Sq Pth
P
Thames Path
Cow Lane
E F
Richfield Av
Tessa Rd
Trafford
Road
Cremyll Rd
33
71
Field Aver
Randolph
Newport
Rd
York Rd
Drigant
Swansea
Ross Rd
CAVERSHAM ROAD
A4074 BRIDGE
Caversham
Bridge
The Willows
Thames Path
Promenade
Abbotsmead
Pl
College
St
Stephens
Rd
Cardinal
Cl
Harley
Rd
Prim Sch
Wolsey
Patrick Rd
Elliots
Way
Gosbrook
Road
Westfield Rd
Washington Rd
St Annes RC
Primary
School
A4074
CHURCH ST
P
PO
P
Rectory
North St
South St
Chester St
Short
St
Hampden
Rd
GEORGE STREET
ARCHER ROAD
GOSBROOK RO
King's Road
Queen's Road
72
5
St John's
St Mar
Mon

Frys
Island
Thames
Tamesis
**Christchurch
Meadows
Playing
Field**
Hills
Meadow
G H

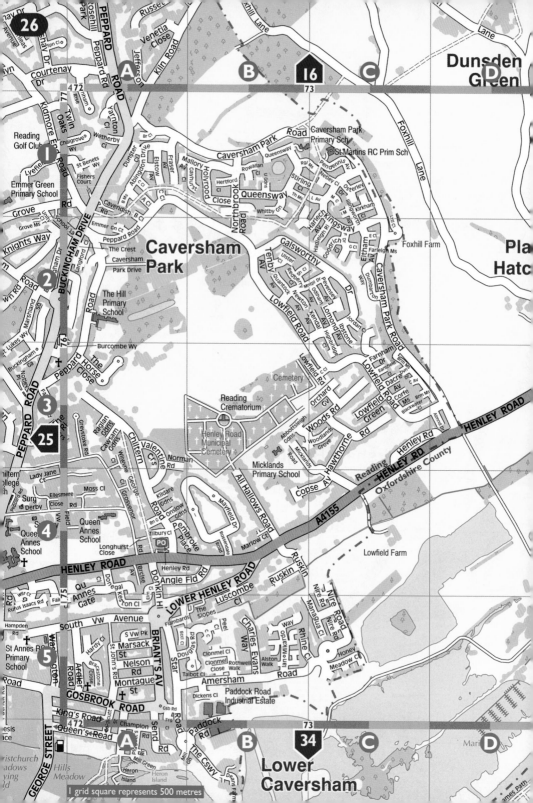

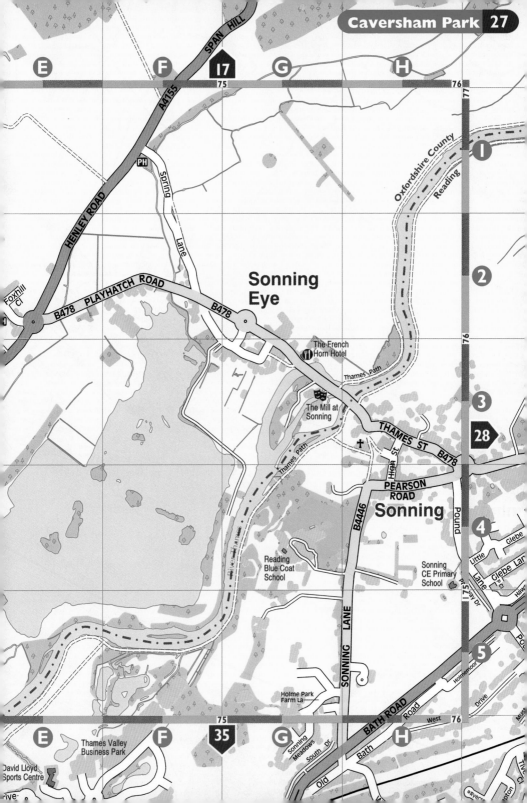

E F **17** G H

SPAN HILL

A4155

HENLEY ROAD

PH

Spring Lane

Oxfordshire County

Reading

B478 PLAYHATCH ROAD

Foxhill Cl

B478

Sonning Eye

The French Horn Hotel

Thames Path

The Mill at Sonning

THAMES ST

B478

28

Thames Path

PEARSON ROAD

High St

Sonning

B4446

Reading Blue Coat School

Sonning CE Primary School

Pound Lane

Little Lane

Glebe

Glebe Lane

A4155 Dr

SONNING LANE

Holme Park Farm La

BATH ROAD

Bath Road West

Holmemoor Drive

Drive

E F **35** G H

Thames Valley Business Centre

David Lloyd Sports Centre

Sonning Meadows

South Dr

Old Bath

75 76 77

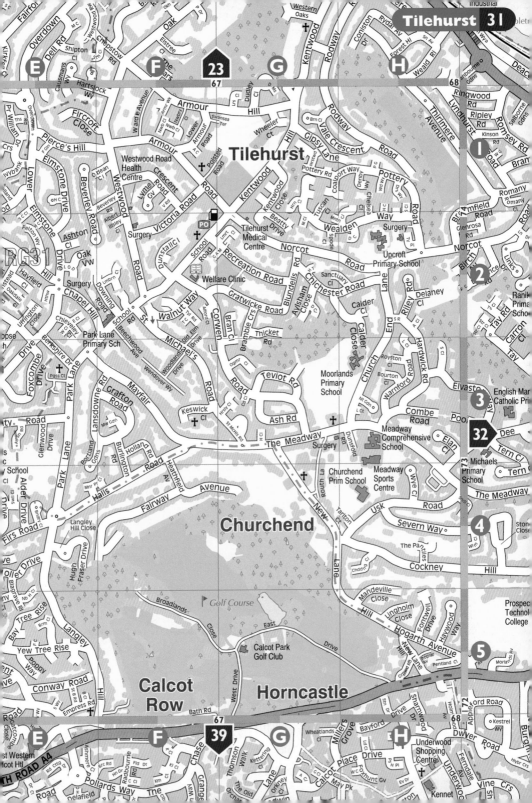

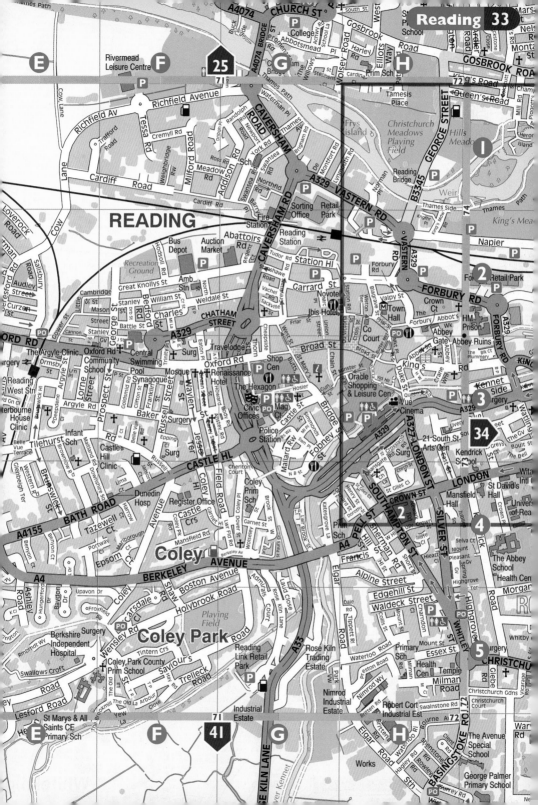

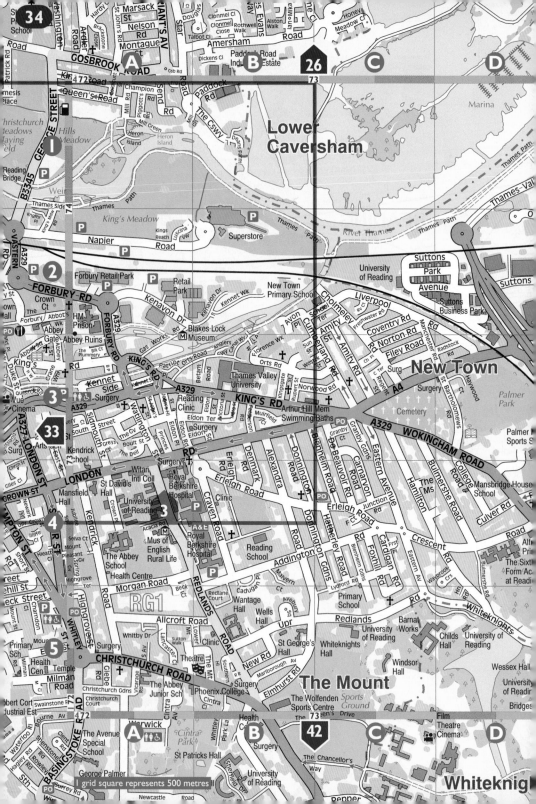

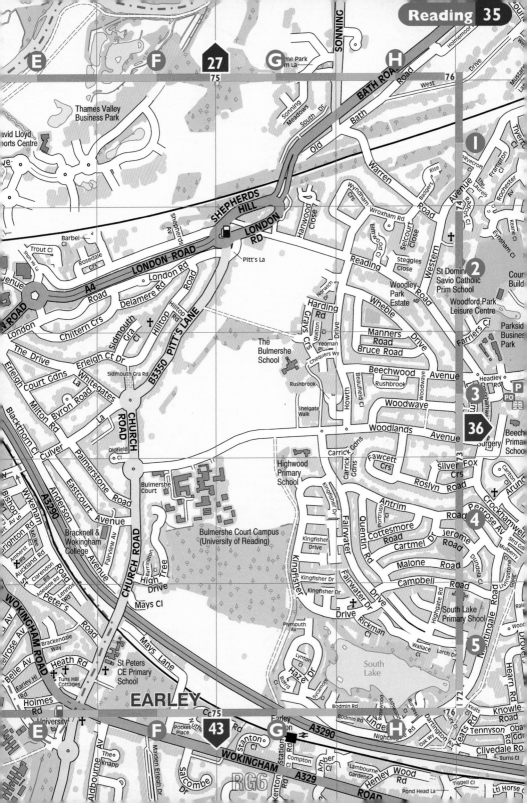

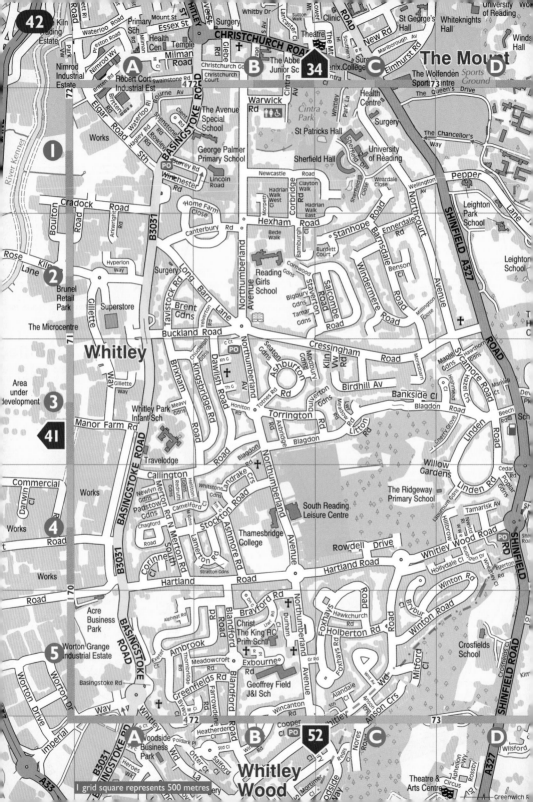

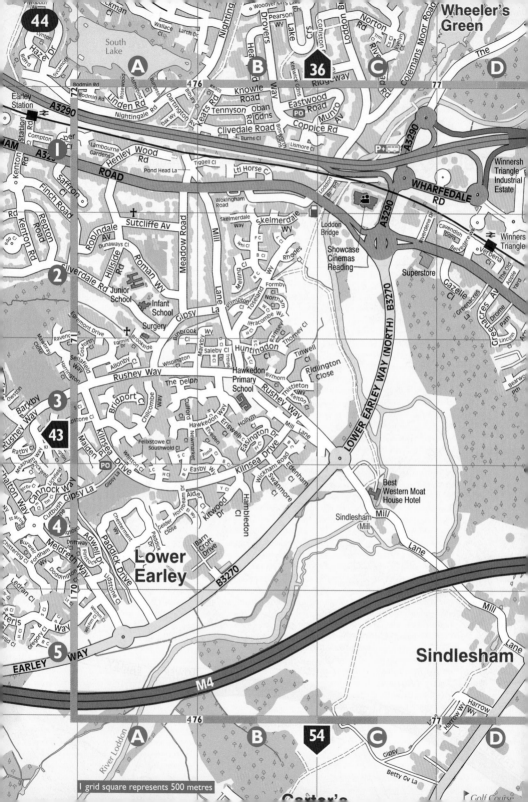

E 82 F 83 72

Windsor and Maidenhead
Wokingham

G H

Straight Mile Farm

I

Carter's Hill

Road

Maidenhead

Marchfield House

2

Green Lane

71

BINF

B30

Kingscote

3

Roughgrove Copse

AD

Ashridge Manor

Warren House Road

Rushton's Farm

Binfield Road

Bracknell Forest
Wokingham

4

170

Stokes Farm

5

green

Warren House Rd

Green Croft

Road

Ashridge

Pigott Rd

Dowles Grn

Hutsons Cl

Eustace Crescent

Whaley Rd

Child Cl

Moores Green

Blake Cl

sorrel

Macphail Cl

Rosebay

Pavley Drive

Webb Ct

Comfrey Cl

Montague Close

Way

Crs

ney

Budge's Road

82

Budge's Gdns

Keephatch Rd

Sundew Cl

Cl

Trefoil Cll

57

Keep Hatch

83

E F G H

Surgery

The Palmer CE Junior School

Keep Hatch Primary School

Clover

Hughes Rd

Monkshood

wcross Road

Willow

Dyer Rd

d Road

A329(M)

48

South Dr
South Drive

A   **B**   **C**   **D**

Trash C

464

69

65

Home Farm

Jaques's

Folly

Whiteh

Kingston

Lane

1

Sulhamstead

Lane

St Michaels Lane

Sulhamstead Bannister Upper End

Lane

Road

2

Folly

68

White's

Hill

†

Sulhamstead Abbots

3

Lane

Sulhamstead Road

Sulhamstead & Ufton Nervet Primary School

†

Ufton Nervet

Sulhamstead Road

Ash Lane

Bluebell Dr

Hunter's Hill

Southwood Gdns

Pinchcut

Omer's Ri

Omer's Rise

4

Lane

Shortheath

Wise's Firs

Bluebell Drive

Abbey Pk

Clayhill Road

Woodlands Rd Ridge

Garland Junior School

Stabl

Alder Gld

Woodman's Lane

Krk Crs

Loie's

Birch

Lane

Warren Cl

Fox Cl

Pine Ridge Road

Oakc

Camp Road

167

Green

5

RG7

Benham's Farm

Acorn Gdns

Jordan's La

Bannister Rd

Mrs Blands Infant School

Willink Leisure Centre

School Lane

Goodwood Cl

Recreation Rd

Fir's End

Bung

Willink School

Park

PO

Firlands

Bland's Close

Oak Dr

Garlands VW Cl

Hollybush

Palmer's Lane

† Bur

464

A   **B**   ▼**58**   **C**   **D**

Totterdown

65

Tanner's Cl

Lane

Sun Gdns

Three Firs Way

Three Firs Way

Brocas

Lane

1 grid square represents 500 metres

E F G H

66 67 69

Bennett's

Green Farm

Theale Road

Burghfield St Marys Primary School

School Rd

Hatch La

Church Lane

I

Sulhamstead Road

Burghfield

Reading Road

Willow Cl

Post Office Lane

2

Hazel Close

Clayhill Road

Elm Dr

Rowan Way

Sycamore Cl

Burghfield Place

68

The Mearings

Chestnut Cl

Hillfields

3

Reading Road

James's Lane

50

Highwoods

Hillside

Kestrel Wy

Barn Owl Wy

Lamden Way

Finch Cl

Thrush Way

Chaffinch Wy

Hannington's Way

Burghfield Hill

St Mary Myrtle

W St Mr W

C C

James's Lane

A167

Graze Green

4

Burghfield Health Centre

Hermits Cl

Tarragon Way

Man's Hill

Culverlands

Pembroke Close

Tarragon Way

Chervil Way

Great Auclum

Goring Lane

5

Lane

isset ield

Common

E F G H

66 67

Goring Lane

59

Goddard's Green

Oakfield

Pier

g Lane

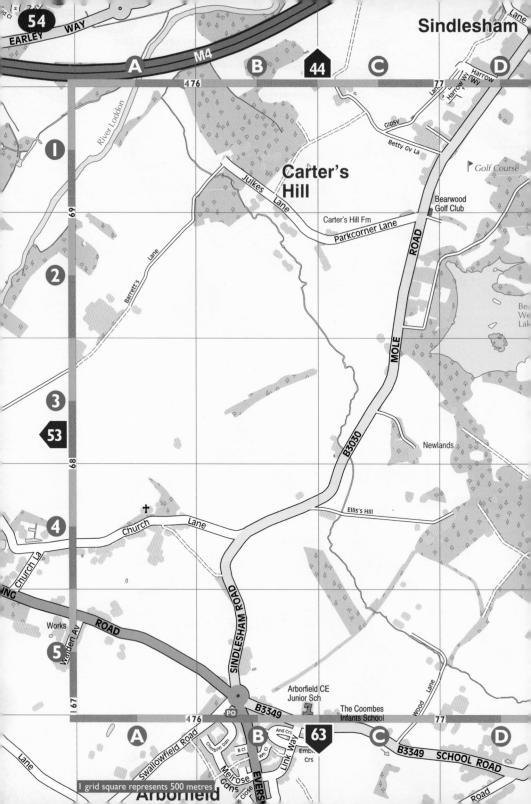

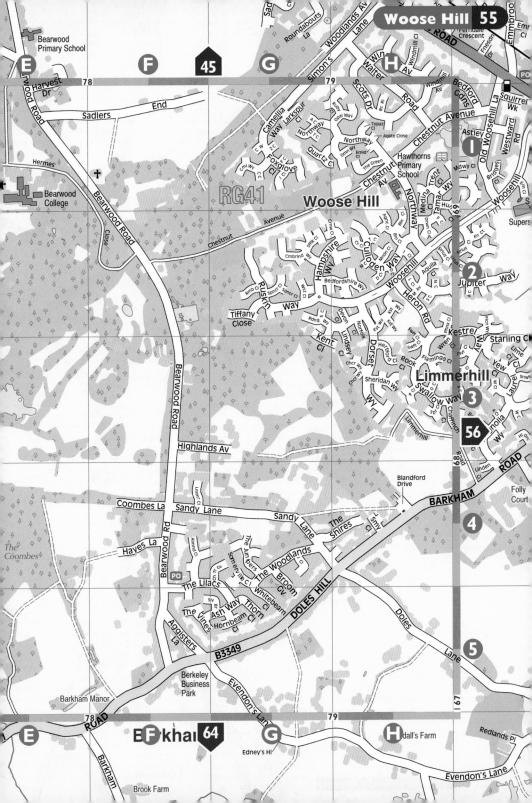

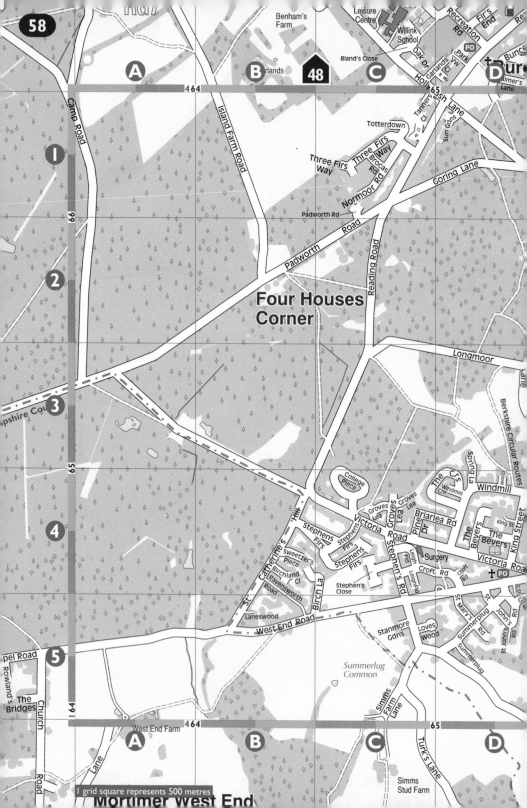

E

F

49

G

H

66

67

Great Auclum

usset Gld

mon

Goring Lane

Goddard's Green

Oakfield

Lockram Lane

New Road

I

ng Lane

Lockram Lane

66

Berkshire Circular Routes

Warennes Wood

Sawyer's Ley

Wokefield Rw

Wokefield Park Golf Club

Mortimer Park

2

Golf Course

Brewery Common

Mann's Farm

Mortimer Lane

Mortimer House

3

65

Nightingale Lane

4

Hammonds Heath

Wheat's Farm

Berkshire Circular Routes

The Street

Tayberry Lov

Strawberry Flds

mer

The Street

Orchard Road

The Avenue

Monktons La

5

The Avenue

Kiln Lane

The Avenue

Mortimer Lodge

Gordon Palmer Cl

Mortimer St Marys CE Junior Sch

The Street

Church Farm Barns

Stratfield Mortimer

Mortimer Station

Station Road

I 64

The

E

F

G

H

66

67

Berkshire Circular Routes

Lane

E   F   52   G   H
73   74

Croft Road

Lane

High
Copse Fa

R

E

Hyde
End

ROAD

Hyde End Rd

I

Moor
Copse

Winston Cl

Sussex La

1

centur Dr

67

Lansdowne
Gdns

Jordan
Cl

2

99

Nutter's

Great
Wood

Lane

3

River Loddon

Swallowfield
Park

62   Swallowfield Rd

4

Swallowfield Road

The Street

165

Hornbeams

Surgery

Swallowfield

5

The Street

PO

Culvs Wy

C
Wy

The
Naylors

Foxborough

Part Lane

Brookside
Business
Centre

PH

Rowe's Farm

Lane

Trowe's

73   74

harlto

E   F   G   H
Lane

Cemetery

Ⓐ   Ⓑ   53   Ⓒ   Ⓓ

474   67   75

1

Moor Copse

2

Nutter's

69

3

Great Wood

61

Tanner's Farm

Swallowfield Road

4

65

Swallowfield Road

Kiln Hill

5

Swallowfield

Bungler's Hill

474   75

Ⓐ   Ⓑ   Ⓒ   Ⓓ

Greensward

Lane

Swallowfield Road

White's Farm

Swallowfield Road

Castle Hill

Road

The chatters

Church

Lane

Walden A

Swallow

Arb Cro

Arborfield Court

Parsons Farm

Farley Court

Farley Hill Primary

Fa

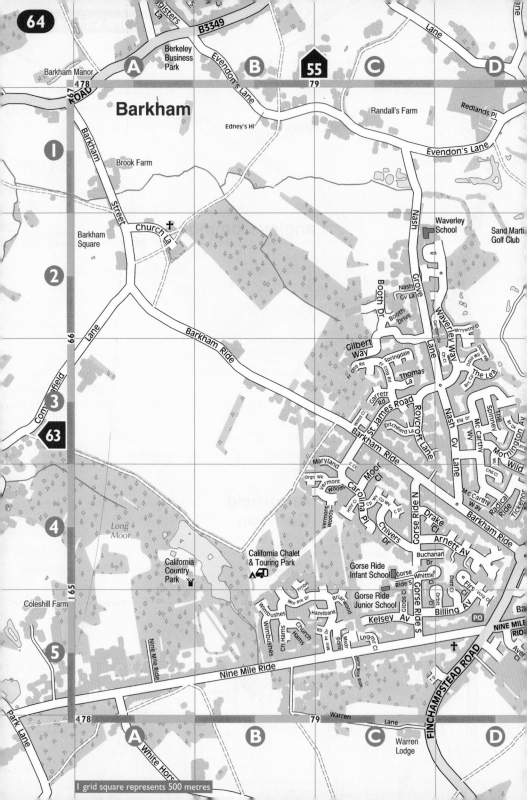

Schools address data provided by Education Direct.

Petrol station information supplied by Johnsons

One-way street data provided by © Tele Atlas N.V. Tele Atlas

Garden centre information provided by

Garden Centre Association Britains best garden centres

Wyevale Garden Centres

The statement on the front cover of this atlas is sourced, selected and quoted
from a reader comment and feedback form received in 2004

How do I find the perfect place?